MAKE ME LAUGH!

HOLIDAY HOWLERS

JOKES FOR PUNNY PARTIES

by Peter and Connie Roop
pictures by Brian Gable

Carolrhoda Books, Inc. • Minneapolis

Q: What do cats say on New Year's Eve?

A: "Happy Mew Year."

Q: What musical instruments do skeletons play?

A: Trom-bones.

Q: What did Santa say on Christmas Eve?

A: "That wraps it up for another year."

Q: What is the best thing to put in a birthday cake?

A: Your teeth.

Q: How do you call a skeleton?

A: On the telebone.

Q: What happened when witches look alike?

A: You don't know which witch is which.

Q: Why won't Santa give you five cents?

A: Because he's Nickle-less.

Q: What kind of tape do you use on Halloween?

A: Mask-ing tape.

Q: What's a favorite ghost dance?

A: Boo-gie woogie.

Q: Where do ghouls stay on vacation?

A: At the gobl-inn.

Q: What does Santa do when his reindeer make a sloppy landing on a housetop?

A: He hits the roof.

Q: What do you find at the beach on Halloween?

A: Sand-witches.

Q: When do pigs like to play in the dirt?

A: Ground Hog's Day.

Q: What goes "crack, crack, whoosh, pop, scared ya"?

A: A ghost chewing booble gum.

Q: When Santa Claus is flying over your town, what does he see on his right hand?

A: His mitten.

Q: What did Abraham Lincoln do with his boots after he wore them out?

A: He wore them back in again.

Q: Why do skeletons laugh so much?

A: They have funny bones.

Q: What does a baseball pitcher do on his birthday?

A: He throws a party.

Q: What holiday do werewolves like best?

A: Howl-oween.

Q: What kind of key do you use on Thanksgiving?

A: A tur-key.

Q: Which reindeer knows Morse code?

A: Dasher.

Q: How does a witch tell time?

A: She checks her witch watch.

Q: When are ghost stores open?

A: Every day Moanday through Frightday.

Q: Who protects Santa from toy thieves?

A: The North Police.

Q: What do you give a skeleton for Valentine's Day?

A: Bone-bones in a heart-shaped box.

Q: What happens when two valentines fight?

A: A heart is broken.

Q: What do witches sing when they mix their brew?

A: "Some Enchanted Evening."

Q: Why are goats fun to have at a party?

A: They are always kidding around.

Q: What do you when you cross Saint Nicholas with a bear?

A: Santa Claws.

Q: How did the reindeer know that Santa had fallen out of the sleigh?

A: They felt a rein drop.

Q: Why was cupid put in jail?

A: He was caught stealing hearts.

Q: What prize did the ghost win at the fair?

A: A boo ribbon for booberry pie.

Q: What do ghosts like to eat for dinner?

A: Ham-boo-gers and french fright potatoes.

Q: What is a pig's favorite holiday?

A: Valen-swine's Day.

Q: What do witches like to drink?

A: Apple spider.

Q: Who takes presents to young crows?

A: Santa Caws.

Q: What do skeletons like to eat for dinner?

A: Maca-boney and cheese.

Q: What do elves like to eat?

A: Elf-elfa.

Q: Who brings presents to baby sand crabs?

A: Sandy Claws.

Q: Why did the goat crash the party?

A: She was always butting in.

Q: What do ghosts like to drink?

A: Le-moan-ade.

Q: What kind of knot does Santa use to tie up his reindeer?

A: A rein-bow knot.

Q: Why is a pig's birthday party so much fun?

A: Everyone goes hog wild.

Q: What do ghosts and goblins eat for lunch?

A: Peanut boo-ter sand-witches.

Q: Which reindeer is a ball of fire?

A: Comet.

Q: Which burns longer, candles on a birthday cake or candles in a candlestick?

A: Neither. They both burn shorter.

Q: What do ghosts like to eat for dessert?
A: Ice scream.

Q: What do reindeer do when polar bears chase them?
A: They run for deer life.

Q: What did one birthday candle say to the other?
A: "These birthdays really burn me up!"

Q: What song do werewolves sing at Christmas?
A: "Deck the Howls with Bow-wows of Howly."

Q: What's fast and red and goes, "Oh, oh, oh!"?
A: Santa Claus flying backward.

Q: How did the mother vampire know her little vampire had a cold?
A: She heard him coffin.

Q: What goes, "Ho, ho, ho, OOPS!"?

A: Santa Claus falling out of his sleigh.

Q: What do you say to a lazy Easter bunny?

A: "Hop to it!"

Q: What do you call the fear of getting stuck in a chimney?

A: Santa Claustrophobia.

Q: How does a ghost open the door of a haunted house?

A: She uses a spoo-key.

Q: Who wears a red cap, bounds across Africa, and gives presents to other animals?

A: Santelope.

Q: What does a nearsighted ghost wear so he can see?

A: Spooktacles.

Q: Why did the Egyptian ghost cry?

A: She wanted her mummy.

Q: What's black and white and red all over?

A: Santa Claus riding a zebra.

Q: Why wouldn't the little ghost go to sleep?

A: She wanted her night fright turned on.

Q: Who is covered with feathers, lays eggs, and helps pull Santa's sleigh on Christmas Eve?

A: Rudolph the Red-Nosed Rein Duck.

Q: What do baby ghosts wear on their feet?

A: Boo-ties.

Q: Why does Santa Claus carry presents around the world?

A: Because the presents won't go by themselves.

Q: What's gray, weighs more than 10,000 pounds, and comes down your chimney on Christmas Eve?

A: A noel-ephant.

Q: Why is Easter dinner fun?

A: Because people ham it up.

Q: What do little ghosts do before bedtime?

A: They take boo-ble baths.

Q: How do you find Santa?

A: Follow the Santa Clues.

Q: What does a witch's broom do when it's tired?

A: It goes to sweep.

Q: What does Santa do when he gets soot on his clothes?

A: He puts the clothes in his sootcase.

Mark: Why is Rudolph the Red a good weatherman?

Sally: Why?

Mark: Rudolph the Red knows rain, dear.

Q: Why do ghosts hear so well?

A: Because they're eerie.

Q: What does Santa Claus wear when he dresses up?

A: A Nicktie.

Q: Why did the Thanksgiving cranberries turn red?

A: They saw the turkey dressing.

Q: Why is Father's Day later in the year than Mother's Day?

A: It's "father" away.

Q: What do you call a reindeer that does back flips while flying through the air?

A: A deerdevil.

Q: What does Santa wear all year long?

A: Santa Clothes.

Q: When do ghosts make noise?

A: Every chains they get.

Q: Where does Santa keep his Santa Clothes?

A: In his Santa Closet.

Q: What does a ghost read in bed?

A: A scary boo-k.

Q: What was the turkey doing in the Thanksgiving Day parade?

A: Using his drumsticks.

Q: How did Dancer get his name?

A: When he met Santa Claus, he said, "My name is Daniel, but you can call me Dan, Sir."

Q: Who was the most famous ghost detective?

A: Sherlock Moans.

Q: Who was the most famous witch detective?

A: Warlock Holmes.

Q: Who was the most famous skeleton detective?

A: Sherlock Bones.

Q: What does Santa have on his fireplace mantle?

A: Saint Nick-nacks.

Q: Why do witches go to the circus?

A: To see the acro-bats.

Q: What is an Easter bunny's favorite sandwich?

A: Peanut butter and jelly beans.

Q: Who makes scary movies about Santa Claus?

A: Elf-Red Hitchcock.

Q: Where does Christmas come before Thanksgiving?

A: In the dictionary.

Q: How does an owl stop?

A: It comes to a screeching halt.

Q: What do you call a ghost pirate?

A: A boo-caneer.

Q: If stockings are filled with presents on Christmas Eve, what are they filled with the rest of the year?

A: Feet.

Q: What is a vampire's favorite holiday?

A: Fangsgiving.

Q: What did the witch say about her trip to the beauty shop?

A: It was a hair-raising experience.

Q: What do you eat with soup on the Fourth of July?

A: Fire crackers.

Q: Who is the most famous French skeleton?

A: Napoleon Bone-aparte.

Q: What do the elves listen to while they work?

A: Gift rap music.

Q: What makes more noise than a firecracker?

A: Two firecrackers.

Q: Which building does Dracula visit in New York?

A: The Vampire State Building.

Q: Who is Santa's favorite singer?
A: Elves Presley.

Q: Where do most goblins live?
A: In North and South Scarolina.

Q: Where do you go to learn to be an elf?
A: To Santa Class.

Q: What's the first thing you learn at Santa Class?
A: The elfabet.

Q: Where do most werewolves live?
A: Howlywood, California.

Q: What do hogs do on Labor Day?
A: Go on pig-nics.

Q: What do you say to a skeleton leaving on a long cruise?
A: "Bone voyage!"

Q: How do you bargain with a witch?

A: You hag-gle.

Q: How do Santa's elves get over the fence into the reindeer pen?

A: They do the North Pole Vault.

Q: What was the first bus to cross the Atlantic Ocean?

A: Colum-bus.

Q: What do you call the furry coats monsters wear?

A: Wolf-wear.

Q: Where do you go to celebrate Election Day?

A: Political parties.

Q: What do skeletons wear in the sun?

A: Sun bone-ets.

Q: What does a firecracker do when it's angry?

A: Blows its top.

Q: Why is turkey a good holiday food?

A: You can gobble it up.

Q: Why did Holly miss school on her birthday?

A: She heard it was a Holly-day.

Q: What do you call a rancher ghost?

A: A boo-ckaroo.

Q: What did the elves say when the reindeer refused to help make the Christmas goodies?

A: "We'll do it ours-elves."

Q: What do you call a hungry dachshund in October?

A: A hollow-weenie.

Q: How do ghouls travel?

A: By flying ghost to ghost.

Q: Where do ghosts go on vacation?

A: Lake Eerie.

Q: What do Santa Claus's children call him?

A: Father Christmas.

Q: What does a ghost do when he gets into a car?

A: He boockles up for safety.

Q: Is "Saint Nicholas" Santa Claus's real name?

A: No, it's his Nick name.

Q: If you go to the North Pole, how do you get Santa to let you in his workshop?

A: Ring the deerbell.

Q: What does a ghost use when she runs out of bus tokens?

A: Loose chains.

Q: What's the first thing Santa Claus does when he gets in his sleigh?

A: He sits down.

Q: What is the best month for a parade?

A: March.

Q: What do witches do when they're tired?

A: They stop for a spell.

Q: Why does Santa Claus come down the chimney?

A: Because he doesn't have the key to the front door.

Q: What kind of music did the Pilgrims like?

A: Plymouth rock.

Q: Who has red cheeks, a belly that shakes when he laughs like a bowl full of jelly, and climbs down your chimney?

A: A fat, jolly, chimney sweep with a cold.

Q: How do witches and ghosts celebrate the Fourth of July?

A: Witches light fire cracklers, and ghosts light spooklers.

Q: What subject are witches best at in school?

A: Spelling.

Q: What did the ghost do when he lost his shoe?

A: He haunted for it.

Q: Where does Santa Claus go when he's done delivering presents?

A: Ho-ho-home.

This book is available in two editions:
Library binding by Carolrhoda Books, Inc.,
    a division of Lerner Publishing Group
Soft cover by First Avenue Editions,
    an imprint of Lerner Publishing Group
241 First Avenue North
Minneapolis, MN 55401 U.S.A.

Website address: www.lernerbooks.com

Library of Congress Cataloging-in-Publication Data

Roop, Peter.
    Holiday howlers : jokes for punny parties / by Peter and Connie Roop ; pictures
by Brian Gable.
        p.   cm. — (Make me laugh)
    Summary: A collection of jokes and riddles about holidays.
    ISBN: 1–57505–645–3 (lib. bdg. : alk. paper)
    ISBN: 1–57505–705–0 (pbk. : alk. paper)
    1. Holidays—Juvenile humor. [1. Holidays—Humor. 2. Jokes. 3. Riddles. 4.
Puns and punning.] I. Roop, Connie. II. Gable, Brian, 1949– ill. III. Title. IV.
Series.
PN6231.H547 R65 2004
818'.5402—dc21   2002151104

Manufactured in the United States of America
1 2 3 4 5 6 – DP – 09 08 07 06 05 04